The Holy Rosary

Introduction
Based on the Apostolic Letter
Rosary of the Virgin Mary
by Saint John Paul II

A Treasury of Christian Prayers
Inspired by Events in the Lives
of Jesus and Mary

MARIAN PRESS
STOCKBRIDGE MA 01263

PRO CHRISTO ET ECCLESIA

2019

IMPRIMI POTEST:
Very Rev. Walter Dziordz, MIC
Superior of the Saint Stanislaus Kostka Province
Marians of the Immaculate Conception
Stockbridge, MA 01263
February 23, 2003

*The NIHIL OBSTAT is a declaration that a book or pamphlet is
considered to be free from doctrinal or moral error. It is not
implied that those who have granted the NIHIL OBSTAT agree
with the contents, opinions, or statements expressed.*

Compiled by: *Stephanie Wilcox-Hughes & David Came*
Editing and Proofreading: *David Came*
Artwork, composition, and layout by: *Jessie Wolska*
Cover art: *Statue of Our Lady of Fatima*

Printed in the United States of America
by *Marian Press*
Stockbridge, Massachusetts 01263

ISBN: 978-0-944203-70-5

Available from:
Marian Helpers Center
Stockbridge, MA 01263

Prayer Line: 1-800-804-3823
marian.org
Order Line: 1-800-462-7426
ShopMercy.org

Contents

Introduction
Based on the Apostolic Letter *Rosary of the Virgin Mary* by St. John Paul II

The Rosary of the Virgin Mary, which gradually took form in the second millennium under the guidance of the Spirit of God, is a prayer loved by countless Saints and encouraged by the Magisterium. Simple yet profound, it still remains, at the dawn of this third millennium, a prayer of great significance, destined to bring forth a harvest of holiness. ...

With the Rosary, the Christian people sits at the school of Mary and is led to contemplate the beauty on the face of Christ and to experience the depths of His love. Through the Rosary the faithful receive abundant grace, as though from the very hands of the Mother of the Redeemer. ...

The most important reason for strongly encouraging the practice of the Rosary is that it represents a most effective means of fostering among the faithful that commitment to the contemplation of the Christian mystery which I have proposed in the Apostolic Letter *Novo Millennio Ineunte* as a genuine "training in holiness": "What is needed is a Christian life distinguished above all in the art of prayer." Inasmuch as contemporary culture – even amid so many indications to the contrary – has witnessed the flowering of a new call for spirituality due also to the influence of other religions, it is more urgent than ever that our Christian communities should become "genuine schools of prayer." ...

Prayer for Peace and for the Family

A number of historical circumstances also make a revival of the Rosary quite timely. First of all, the need to implore from God the gift of peace. The Rosary has many times been proposed by my predecessors and myself as a prayer for peace. At the start of a millennium which began with the terrifying attacks of September 11, 2001 – a millennium which witnesses every day in numerous parts of the world fresh scenes of bloodshed and violence – to rediscover the Rosary means to immerse oneself in contemplation of the mystery of Christ who "is our peace," since He made "the two of us one, and broke down the dividing wall of hostility" (Eph 2:14). Consequently, one cannot recite the Rosary without feeling caught up in a clear commitment to advancing peace, especially in the land of Jesus, still so sorely afflicted and so close to the heart of every Christian.

A similar need for commitment and prayer arises in relation to another critical contemporary issue: the family, the primary cell of society – increasingly menaced by forces of disintegration on both the ideological and practical planes, so as to make us fear for the future of this fundamental and indispensable institution.... . The revival of the Rosary in Christian families, within the context of a broader pastoral ministry to the family, will be an effective aid to countering the devastating effects of this crisis typical of our age.

"Behold, Your Mother!" *(John 19:27)*

Many signs indicate that still today the Blessed Virgin desires to exercise through this same prayer that maternal concern to which the dying Redeemer entrusted, in the person of the beloved disciple, all the sons and daughters of the Church: "Woman, behold your son!" (Jn19:26). Well-known are the occasions in the nineteenth and the twentieth centuries on which the Mother of Christ made her presence felt and her voice heard, in order to exhort the People of God to this form of contemplative prayer. I would mention in particular, on account of their great influence on the lives of Christians and the authoritative recognition they have received from the Church, the apparitions of Lourdes and of Fatima; these shrines continue to be visited by great numbers of pilgrims seeking comfort and hope.

Following the Witnesses

It would be impossible to name all the many Saints who discovered in the Rosary a genuine path to growth in holiness. We need but mention St. Louis Marie Grignion de Montfort, the author of an excellent work on the Rosary, and, closer to ourselves, Padre Pio of Pietrelcina, whom I recently had the joy of canonizing. As a true apostle of the Rosary, Blessed Bartolo Longo had a special charism. His path to holiness rested on an inspiration heard in the depths of his heart: "Whoever spreads the Rosary is saved!"… . By his whole life's work and especially by the practice of the

7

"Fifteen Saturdays," Bartolo Longo promoted the Christocentric and contemplative heart of the Rosary, and received great encouragement and support from Leo XIII, the "Pope of the Rosary."

A Face Radiant as the Sun

"And He was transfigured before them, and His face shone like the sun" (Mt 17:2). The Gospel scene of Christ's transfiguration, in which the three Apostles Peter, James, and John appear entranced by the beauty of the Redeemer, can be seen as an icon of Christian contemplation. To look upon the face of Christ, to recognize its mystery amid the daily events and the sufferings of His human life, and then to grasp the divine splendor definitively revealed in the Risen Lord, seated in glory at the right hand of the Father: this is the task of every follower of Christ and therefore the task of each one of us. In contemplating Christ's face we become open to receiving the mystery of Trinitarian life, experiencing ever anew the love of the Father and delighting in the joy of the Holy Spirit. Saint Paul's words can then be applied to us: "Beholding the glory of the Lord, we are being changed into His likeness, from one degree of glory to another; for this comes from the Lord who is the Spirit" (2 Cor 3:18).

Mary, Model of Contemplation

The contemplation of Christ has an incomparable model in Mary. In a unique way the face of the Son belongs to Mary. It was in her womb that Christ was formed, receiving from her a human resemblance

8

which points to an even greater spiritual closeness. No one has ever devoted himself to the contemplation of the face of Christ as faithfully as Mary. The eyes of her heart already turned to Him at the Annunciation, when she conceived Him by the power of the Holy Spirit.

In the months that followed she began to sense His presence and to picture His features. When at last she gave birth to Him in Bethlehem, her eyes were able to gaze tenderly on the face of her Son, as she "wrapped Him in swaddling cloths, and laid Him in a manger" (Lk 2:7).

Thereafter Mary's gaze, ever filled with adoration and wonder, would never leave Him. At times it would be a questioning look, as in the episode of the finding in the Temple: "Son, why have you treated us so?" (Lk 2:48); it would always be a penetrating gaze, one capable of deeply understanding Jesus, even to the point of perceiving His hidden feelings and anticipating His decisions, as at Cana (cf. Jn 2:5). At other times it would be a look of sorrow, especially beneath the Cross, where her vision would still be that of a mother giving birth, for Mary not only shared the passion and death of her Son, she also received the new son given to her in the beloved disciple (cf. Jn 19:26-27). On the morning of Easter hers would be a gaze radiant with the joy of the Resurrection, and finally, on the day of Pentecost, a gaze afire with the outpouring of the Spirit (cf. Acts 1:14).

Mary's Memories

Mary lived with her eyes fixed on Christ, treasuring His every word: "She kept all these things, pondering them in her heart" (Lk 2:19; cf. 2:51). The memories of Jesus, impressed upon her heart, were always with her, leading her to reflect on the various moments of her life at her Son's side. In a way those memories were to be the "rosary" which she recited uninterruptedly throughout her earthly life.

Even now, amid the joyful songs of the heavenly Jerusalem, the reasons for her thanksgiving and praise remain unchanged. They inspire her maternal concern for the pilgrim Church, in which she continues to relate her personal account of the Gospel. Mary constantly sets before the faithful the "mysteries" of her Son, with the desire that the contemplation of those mysteries will release all their saving power. In the recitation of the Rosary, the Christian community enters into contact with the memories and the contemplative gaze of Mary.

The Rosary, a Contemplative Prayer

The Rosary, precisely because it starts with Mary's own experience, is an exquisitely contemplative prayer. Without this contemplative dimension, it would lose its meaning, as Pope Paul VI clearly pointed out: "Without contemplation, the Rosary is a body without a soul, and its recitation runs the risk of becoming a mechanical repetition of formulas, in violation of the admonition of Christ: 'In praying do not heap up empty phrases as the Gentiles do; for they think they will be heard for their many words' (Mt 6:7). By its nature the recitation of the Rosary calls for a quiet rhythm and a lingering pace, helping the individual to meditate on the mysteries of the Lord's life as seen through the eyes of her who was closest to the Lord. In this way the unfathomable riches of these mysteries are disclosed." It is worth pausing to consider this profound insight of Paul VI, in order to bring out certain aspects of the Rosary which show that it is really a form of Christocentric contemplation.

Remembering Christ with Mary

Mary's contemplation is above all a remembering. We need to understand this word in the biblical sense of remembrance (*zakar*) as a making present of the works brought about by God in the history of salvation. The Bible is an account of saving events culminating in Christ Himself. These events not only belong to "yesterday"; they are also part of the "today" of salvation. This making present comes about above all in the Liturgy: what God accomplished centuries ago did not only affect the direct witnesses of those events; it continues to affect people in every age with its gift of grace. To some extent this is also true of every other devout approach to those events: to "remember" them in a spirit of faith and love is to be open to the grace which Christ won for us by the mysteries of His life, death, and resurrection.

Consequently, while it must be reaffirmed with

the Second Vatican Council that the Liturgy, as the exercise of the priestly office of Christ and an act of public worship, is "the summit to which the activity of the Church is directed and the font from which all its power flows," it is also necessary to recall that the spiritual life "is not limited solely to participation in the liturgy. Christians, while they are called to prayer in common, must also go to their own rooms to pray to their Father in secret (cf. Mt 6:6); indeed, according to the teaching of the Apostle, they must pray without ceasing" (cf. 1 Thes 5:17).

The Rosary, in its own particular way, is part of this varied panorama of "ceaseless" prayer. If the Liturgy, as the activity of Christ and the Church, is a saving action par excellence, the Rosary too, as a "meditation" with Mary on Christ, is a salutary contemplation. By immersing us in the mysteries of the Redeemer's life, it ensures that what He has done and what the liturgy makes present is profoundly assimilated and shapes our existence.

Learning Christ from Mary

Christ is the supreme Teacher, the revealer and the one revealed. It is not just a question of learning what He taught but of "learning Him." In this regard could we have any better teacher than Mary? From the divine standpoint, the Spirit is the interior teacher who leads us to the full truth of Christ (cf. Jn 14:26; 15:26; 16:13). But among creatures no one knows Christ better than Mary; no one can introduce us to a profound knowledge of

His mystery better than His Mother.

The first of the "signs" worked by Jesus – the changing of water into wine at the marriage in Cana – clearly presents Mary in the guise of a teacher, as she urges the servants to do what Jesus commands (cf. Jn 2:5). We can imagine that she would have done likewise for the disciples after Jesus' Ascension, when she joined them in awaiting the Holy Spirit and supported them in their first mission. Contemplating the scenes of the Rosary in union with Mary is a means of learning from her to "read" Christ, to discover His secrets and to understand His message.

This school of Mary is all the more effective if we consider that she teaches by obtaining for us in abundance the gifts of the Holy Spirit, even as she offers us the incomparable example of her own "pilgrimage of faith." As we contemplate each mystery of her Son's life, she invites us to do as she did at the Annunciation: to ask humbly the questions which open us to the light, in order to end with the obedience of faith: "Behold I am the handmaid of the Lord; be it done to me according to your word" (Lk 1:38).

Being Conformed to Christ with Mary

Christian spirituality is distinguished by the disciple's commitment to become conformed ever more fully to His Master (cf. Rom 8:29; Phil 3:10,12). The outpouring of the Holy Spirit in Baptism grafts the believer like a branch onto the vine which is Christ (cf. Jn 15:5) and makes him a member of Christ's mystical Body (cf. 1 Cor 12:12; Rom 12:5). This initial unity, however, calls for a growing assimilation which will increasingly shape the conduct of the disciple in accordance with the "mind" of Christ: "Have this mind among yourselves, which was in Christ Jesus" (Phil 2:5). In the words of the Apostle, we are called "to put on the Lord Jesus Christ" (cf. Rom 13:14; Gal 3:27). ...

In this process of being conformed to Christ in the Rosary, we entrust ourselves in a special way to the maternal care of the Blessed Virgin. She who is both the Mother of Christ and a member of the Church, indeed her "pre-eminent and altogether singular member," is at the same time the "Mother of the Church." As such, she continually brings to birth children for the mystical Body of her Son. She does so through her intercession, imploring upon them the inexhaustible outpouring of the Spirit. Mary is the perfect icon of the motherhood of the Church.

The Rosary mystically transports us to Mary's side as she is busy watching over the human growth of Christ in the home of Nazareth. This enables her to train us and to mold us with the same care, until Christ is "fully formed" in us (cf. Gal 4:19).

This role of Mary, totally grounded in that of Christ and radically subordinated to it, "in no way obscures or diminishes the unique mediation of Christ, but rather shows its power." This is the luminous principle expressed by the Second Vatican Council which I have so powerfully experienced in my own life and have made the basis of my episcopal motto: *Totus Tuus*. The motto is of course inspired by the teaching of Saint Louis Marie Grignion de Montfort, who explained in the following words Mary's role in the process of our configuration to Christ: "Our entire perfection consists in being conformed, united, and consecrated to Jesus Christ. Hence the most perfect of all devotions is undoubtedly that which conforms, unites, and consecrates us most perfectly to Jesus Christ. Now, since Mary is of all creatures the one most conformed to Jesus Christ, it follows that among all devotions that which most consecrates and conforms a soul to our Lord is devotion to Mary, His Holy Mother, and that the more a soul is consecrated to her the more will it be consecrated to Jesus Christ." Never as in the Rosary do the life of Jesus and that of Mary appear so deeply joined. Mary lives only in Christ and for Christ!

Praying to Christ with Mary

Jesus invited us to turn to God with insistence and the confidence that we will be heard: "Ask, and it will be given to you; seek, and you will find; knock, and it will be opened to you" (Mt 7:7). The basis for this power of prayer is the goodness of the Father, but also the mediation of Christ Himself (cf. 1 Jn 2:1) and the working of the Holy Spirit who "intercedes for us" according to the will of God (cf. Rom 8:26-27). For "we do not know how to pray as we ought" (Rom 8:26), and at times we are not heard "because we ask wrongly" (cf. Jas 4:2-3).

In support of the prayer which Christ and the Spirit cause to rise in our hearts, Mary intervenes with her maternal intercession. "The prayer of the Church is sustained by the prayer of Mary." If Jesus, the one Mediator, is the Way of our prayer, then Mary, His purest and most transparent reflection, shows us the Way. "Beginning with Mary's unique cooperation with the working of the Holy Spirit, the Churches developed their prayer to the Holy Mother of God, centering it on the person of Christ manifested in His mysteries." At the wedding of Cana the Gospel clearly shows the power of Mary's intercession as she makes known to Jesus the needs of others: "They have no wine" (Jn 2:3).

The Rosary is both meditation and supplication. Insistent prayer to the Mother of God is based on confidence that her maternal intercession can obtain all things from the Heart of her Son. She is "all-powerful by grace," to use the bold expression, which needs to be properly understood, of Bl. Bartolo Longo in his Supplication to Our Lady. This is a conviction which, beginning with the Gospel, has grown ever more firm in the experience of the Christian people. ...

When in the Rosary we plead with Mary, the sanctuary of the Holy Spirit (cf. Lk 1:35), she intercedes for us before the Father who filled her with grace and before the Son born of her womb, praying with us and for us.

Proclaiming Christ with Mary

The Rosary is also a path of proclamation and increasing knowledge, in which the mystery of Christ is presented again and again at different levels of the Christian experience. Its form is that of a prayerful and contemplative presentation, capable of forming Christians according to the Heart of Christ. When the recitation of the Rosary combines all the elements needed for an effective meditation, especially in its communal celebration in parishes and shrines, it can present a significant catechetical opportunity which pastors should use to advantage.

In this way too Our Lady of the Rosary continues her work of proclaiming Christ. The history of the Rosary shows how this prayer was used in particular by the Dominicans at a difficult time for the Church due to the spread of heresy. Today we are facing new challenges. Why should we not once more have recourse to the Rosary, with the same faith as those who have gone before us? The Rosary retains all its power and continues to be a valuable pastoral resource for every good evangelizer.

From the Vatican, on the 16th day of October in the year 2002, the beginning of the twenty-fifth year of my Pontificate

John Paul II

FIRST JOYFUL MYSTERY

Fruit of the Mystery:
Humility

The Annunciation

In the sixth month the angel Gabriel was sent from God to a city of Galilee named Nazareth, to a virgin betrothed to a man whose name was Joseph, of the house of David; and the virgin's name was Mary. And he came to her and said, "Hail, full of grace, the Lord is with you!" But she was greatly troubled at the saying, and considered in her mind what sort of greeting this might be. And the angel said to her, "Do not be afraid, Mary, for you have found favor with God. And behold, you will conceive in your womb and bear a son, and you shall call His name Jesus."

- LUKE 1:26-31

Pray 1 "Our Father" – 10 "Hail Marys" – 1 "Glory Be"

Prayer:

> Mary, you received with deep humility
> the news of the Angel Gabriel
> that you were to be
> the Mother of the Son of God.
> Grant that I may always accept the
> will of God with humility like yours.
> Amen.

SECOND JOYFUL MYSTERY

Fruit of the Mystery:
Love of Neighbor

The Visitation

In those days Mary arose and went with haste into the hill country, to a city of Judah, and she entered the house of Zechariah and greeted Elizabeth. And when Elizabeth heard the greeting of Mary, the babe leaped in her womb; and Elizabeth was filled with the Holy Spirit and she exclaimed with a loud cry, "Blessed are you among women, and blessed is the fruit of your womb! And why is this granted me, that the mother of my Lord should come to me? For behold, when the voice of your greeting came to my ears, the babe in my womb leaped for joy. And blessed is she who believed that there would be a fulfillment of what was spoken to her from the Lord!"

- LUKE 1:39-45

Pray 1 "Our Father" – 10 "Hail Marys" – 1 "Glory Be"

Prayer:

Mary, you showed true charity
in visiting Elizabeth
and remaining with her for three months
before the birth of John the Baptist.
Grant me the grace to support
and love my neighbor.
Amen.

THIRD JOYFUL MYSTERY

Fruit of the Mystery:
Poverty of Spirit

The Birth of Jesus

In those days a decree went out from Caesar Augustus that all the world should be enrolled. This was the first enrollment, when Quirinius was governor of Syria. And all went to be enrolled, each to his own city. And Joseph also went up from Galilee, from the city of Nazareth, to Judea, to the city of David, which is called Bethlehem, because he was of the house and lineage of David, to be enrolled with Mary, his betrothed, who was with child. And while they were there, the time came for her to be delivered. And she gave birth to her first-born son and wrapped Him in swaddling cloths, and laid Him in a manger, because there was no place for them in the inn.

- LUKE 2:1-7

Pray 1 "Our Father" – 10 "Hail Marys" – 1 "Glory Be"

Prayer:

Mary, you lovingly accepted the poverty
of the stable, although you were to
give birth to our God and Redeemer.
Grant me the grace to endure poverty
when I long for richer things.
Amen.

Fourth Joyful Mystery

Fruit of the Mystery:
Obedience

The Presentation of Jesus

And when the time came for their purification according to the law of Moses, they brought Him up to Jerusalem to present Him to the Lord, as it is written in the law of the Lord: "Every male that opens the womb shall be called holy to the Lord" and to offer a sacrifice according to what is said in the law of the Lord, "a pair of turtledoves, or two young pigeons." Now there was a man in Jerusalem, whose name was Simeon, and this man was righteous and devout, looking for the consolation of Israel, and the Holy Spirit was upon him. And it had been revealed to him by the Holy Spirit that he should not see death before he had seen the Lord's Christ. And inspired by the Spirit he came into the temple; and when the parents brought in the child Jesus, to do for Him according to the custom of the law, he took Him up in his arms and blessed God and said, "Lord, now lettest thou Thy servant depart in peace, according to Thy word; for mine eyes have seen Thy salvation which Thou has prepared in the presence of all peoples, a light for revelation to the Gentiles, and for glory to Thy people Israel."

- LUKE 2:22-32

Pray 1 "Our Father" – 10 "Hail Marys" – 1 "Glory Be"

Prayer:

Mary, you observed the law of God
in presenting the Child Jesus in the temple.
Help me to grow in the virtue of obedience.
Amen.

FIFTH JOYFUL MYSTERY

Fruit of the Mystery:
Joy in Finding Jesus

Finding the Child Jesus in the Temple

And when He was twelve years old, they went up according to custom; and when the feast was ended, as they were returning, the boy Jesus stayed behind in Jerusalem. His parents did not know it, but supposing Him to be in the company they went a day's journey, and they sought Him among their kinsfolk and acquaintances; and when they did not find Him, they returned to Jerusalem, seeking Him. After three days they found Him in the temple, sitting among the teachers, listening to them and asking them questions; and all who heard Him were amazed at His understanding and His answers. And when they saw Him they were astonished; and His mother said to Him, "Son, why have you treated us so? Behold, Your father and I have been looking for You anxiously." And He said to them, How is it that you sought Me? Did you not know that I must be in My Father's house? And they did not understand the saying which He spoke to them. And He went down with them and came to Nazareth, and was obedient to them; and His mother kept all these things in her heart.

- LUKE 2:42-51

Pray 1 "Our Father" – 10 "Hail Marys" – 1 "Glory Be"

Prayer:

Mary, you were filled with sorrow
at the loss of Jesus, your Son,
and overwhelmed with joy in finding Him
in the temple surrounded by the teachers.
Obtain for me the joy
of staying close to Jesus.
Amen.

First Luminous Mystery

Fruit of the Mystery:
Openness to the Holy Spirit

Baptism of Jesus

Then Jesus came from Galilee to the Jordan to John to be baptized by him. John would have prevented Him, saying, "I need to be baptized by You, and do You come to me?" ... And when Jesus was baptized, He went up immediately from the water, and behold the heavens were opened and He saw the Spirit of God descending like a dove, and alighting on Him; and lo, a voice from heaven, saying, "This is My beloved Son, with whom I am well pleased."

- MATTHEW 3:13-14, 16-17

Pray 1 "Our Father" – 10 "Hail Marys" – 1 "Glory Be"

Prayer:

Jesus, at Your Baptism,
You remained open to the Holy Spirit
and were filled with the power of God
to begin Your public ministry.
Through my Baptism and Confirmation,
may I remain ever open
to the Spirit of God in my life.
Amen.

Fruit of the Mystery:
To Jesus through Mary

Wedding at Cana

On the third day there was a marriage at Cana in Galilee, and the mother of Jesus was there; Jesus also was invited to the marriage, with His disciples. When the wine failed the mother of Jesus said to Him, "They have no wine." … His mother said to the servants, "Do whatever He tells you." … Jesus said to [the servants], "Fill the jars with water." And they filled them to the brim. He said to them, "Now draw some out and take it to the steward of the feast. So they took it. When the steward of the feast tasted the water now become wine … [he] called to the bridegroom and said to him, "Every man serves the good wine first … but you have kept the good wine until now."

- JOHN 2:1-3, 5, 7-10

Pray 1 "Our Father" – 10 "Hail Marys" – 1 "Glory Be"

Prayer:

Mary, you know my needs and the needs
of all your spiritual children so well.
When life is hard
and I face a difficult situation,
please pray to Jesus on my behalf.
Help me to follow your counsel
by doing whatever He tells me.
Amen.

Fruit of the Mystery:
Repentance and Trust in God

Proclaiming the Kingdom

Now after John was arrested, Jesus came into Galilee, preaching the gospel of God and saying, "The time is fulfilled and the kingdom of God is at hand; repent and believe in the gospel." … And they were astonished at His teaching, for He taught them as one who had authority, and not as the scribes. … And He went throughout all Galilee, preaching in their synagogues and casting out demons.

- MARK 1:14-15, 22, 39

Pray 1 "Our Father" – 10 "Hail Marys" – 1 "Glory Be"

Prayer:

Lord Jesus, You came
as the Light into the world,
proclaiming the Good News.
With great boldness and power,
You dispelled the darkness of sin,
death, and the Evil One in the world.
Help me to repent of my own sin
and to trust more in You.
Amen.

Fourth Luminous Mystery

Fruit of the Mystery:
Desire for Holiness

Transfiguration

And after six days Jesus took with Him Peter and James and John and led them up a high mountain apart by themselves; and He was transfigured before them. ... And there appeared to them Elijah with Moses; and they were talking to Jesus. ... And a cloud overshadowed them, and a voice came out of the cloud, "This is My beloved Son; listen to Him."

- MARK 9:2, 4, 7

Pray 1 "Our Father" – 10 "Hail Marys" – 1 "Glory Be"

Prayer:

Lord Jesus, You revealed Your glory
to encourage the disciples
to fix their eyes upon the hope of glory
when faced with trials.
Help me, Lord, to fix my eyes
upon You in the glory of Heaven.
Fill me with the desire to become a saint.
Amen.

Fruit of the Mystery:
Adoration

Institution of the Eucharist

And when the hour came, He sat at table, and the apostles with Him. And He said to them, "I have earnestly desired to eat this passover with you before I suffer." … And He took bread, and when He had given thanks He broke it and gave it to them, saying, "This is My body which is given for you. Do this in remembrance of Me." And likewise the cup after supper, saying, "This cup which is poured out for you is the new covenant in My blood."

- LUKE 22:14-15, 19-20

Pray 1 "Our Father" – 10 "Hail Marys" – 1 "Glory Be"

Prayer:

Lord Jesus, as I am nourished by
your Body and Blood in Holy Communion,
help me to be transformed more
and more into Your image.
And may I spend time adoring You —
Body and Blood, Soul and Divinity —
in the Most Blessed Sacrament.
Amen.

First Sorrowful Mystery

Fruit of the Mystery:
Sorrow for Sin

The Agony in the Garden

And He came out, and went, as was His custom, to the Mount of Olives; and the disciples followed Him. And when He came to the place He said to them, "Pray that you may not enter into temptation." And He withdrew from them about a stone's throw, and knelt down and prayed, "Father, if Thou art willing, remove this cup from Me; nevertheless not My will, but Thine, be done." And there appeared to Him an angel from heaven, strengthening Him. And being in an agony He prayed more earnestly; and His sweat became like great drops of blood falling down upon the ground. And when He rose from prayer, He came to the disciples and found them sleeping for sorrow, and He said to them, "Why do you sleep? Rise and pray that you may not enter into temptation."

- LUKE 22:39-46

Pray 1 "Our Father" – 10 "Hail Marys" – 1 "Glory Be"

Prayer:

Jesus, You suffered a bitter agony
in the Garden of Gethsemane
because of our sins.
Lead me to prayer in my time of need
and grant me true contrition for my sins.
Amen.

Fruit of the Mystery:
Purity

The Scourging at the Pillar

Pilate said to Him, "So You are a king?" Jesus answered, "You say that I am a king. For this I was born, and for this I have come into the world, to bear witness to the truth. Every one who is of the truth hears My voice." Pilate said to Him, "What is truth?" After he had said this, he went out to the Jews again, and told them, "I find no crime in Him. But you have a custom that I should release one man for you at the Passover; will you have me release for you the King of the Jews?" They cried out again, "Not this man, but Barabbas!" Now Barabbas was a robber. Then Pilate took Jesus and scourged Him.

- JOHN 18:37-40; 19: 1

Pray 1 "Our Father" – 10 "Hail Marys" – 1 "Glory Be"

Prayer:

Jesus, You remained pure of heart even
when Your flesh was torn and scourged
by those who hated You.
Help me to grow in the virtue
of purity even when I suffer.
Amen.

THIRD SORROWFUL MYSTERY

Fruit of the Mystery:
Courage

The Crowning with Thorns

Then the soliders of the governor took Jesus into the praetorium, and they gathered the whole battalion before Him. And they stripped Him and put a scarlet robe upon Him, and plaiting a crown of thorns they put it on His head, and put a reed in His right hand. And kneeling before Him they mocked Him, saying, "Hail, King of the Jews!" And they spat on Him, and took the reed and struck Him on the head. And when they had mocked Him, they stripped Him of the robe, and put His own clothes on Him, and led Him away to crucify Him.

- MATTHEW 27:27-31

Pray 1 "Our Father" – 10 "Hail Marys" – 1 "Glory Be"

Prayer:

Jesus, You patiently endured the pain
from the crown of sharp thorns
that was forced upon Your head.
Grant me the strength
to have moral courage to follow You.
Amen.

FOURTH SORROWFUL MYSTERY

Fruit of the Mystery:
Patience

The Carrying of the Cross

As they were marching out, they came upon a man of Cyrene, Simon by name; this man they compelled to carry His cross. And when they came to a place called Golgotha (which means the Place of the Skull), they offered Him wine to drink, mingled with gall; but when He tasted it, He would not drink it.

- MATTHEW 27:32-34

Pray 1 "Our Father" – 10 "Hail Marys" – 1 "Glory Be"

Prayer:

Jesus, You willingly carried Your Cross
for love of Your Father and all people.
Grant me forbearance and patience
to carry my cross in difficult moments.
Amen.

FIFTH SORROWFUL MYSTERY

Fruit of the Mystery:
Perseverance

The Crucifixion of Our Lord Jesus Christ

It was now about the sixth hour, and there was darkness over the whole land until the ninth hour, while the sun's light failed, and the curtain of the temple was torn in two. Then Jesus, crying with a loud voice said, "Father, into Thy hands I commit My spirit!" And having said this He breathed his last. Now when the centurion saw what had taken place, he praised God and said, "Certainly this man was innocent!"

- LUKE 23:44-47

Pray 1 "Our Father" – 10 "Hail Marys" – 1 "Glory Be"

Prayer:

Jesus, You bravely endured torture
on the Cross and gave up Your life
for the salvation of all humankind.
Grant me peace of mind,
body, and spirit, and the grace
of perseverance in adversity.
Amen.

First Glorious Mystery

Fruit of the Mystery:
Faith

The Resurrection of Our Lord Jesus Christ

Mary stood weeping outside the tomb, and as she wept she stooped to look into the tomb; and she saw two angels in white sitting where the body of Jesus had lain, one at the head and one at the feet... She turned around and saw Jesus standing, but she did not know that it was Jesus. Jesus said to her, "Woman, why are you weeping? Whom do you seek?" Supposing Him to be the gardener, she said to Him, "Sir, if you have carried Him away, tell me where you have laid Him, and I will take Him away." Jesus said to her, "Mary." She turned and said to Him in Hebrew, "Rabboni!" (which means Teacher). Jesus said to her, "...go to My brethren and say to them, I am ascending to My Father and your Father, to My God and your God."

- JOHN 20:11-12, 14-17

Pray 1 "Our Father" – 10 "Hail Marys" – 1 "Glory Be"

Prayer:

Jesus, You rose from the dead
in triumph and remained for forty days
with Your disciples,
instructing and encouraging them.
Grant me the desire to always
have faith in You, my Risen Lord.
Amen.

SECOND GLORIOUS MYSTERY

Fruit of the Mystery:
Hope

The Ascension of Our Lord Jesus Christ

As [the apostles] were looking on, [Jesus] was lifted up, and a cloud took Him out of their sight. And while they were gazing into heaven as He went, behold, two men stood by them in white robes and said: "Men of Galilee, why do you stand looking into heaven. This Jesus, who was taken from you into heaven, will come in the same way as you saw Him go into heaven." Then they returned to Jerusalem from the mount called Olivet, which is near Jerusalem, a sabbath day's journey away; and when they had entered, they went to the upper room, where they were staying.

- ACTS 1:9-13

Pray 1 "Our Father" – 10 "Hail Marys" – 1 "Glory Be"

Prayer:

Jesus, You instilled in the disciples
the virtue of hope in life everlasting
and commanded them to carry
Your Gospel throughout the world.
As You sit at the Father's right hand
in heaven, grant me the grace
to grow in the virtue of hope
and inspire me to lead others to You.
Amen.

THIRD GLORIOUS MYSTERY

Fruit of the Mystery:
Love for God

The Descent
of the Holy Spirit

When the day of Pentecost had come, they were all together in one place. And suddenly a sound came from heaven like the rush of a mighty wind, and it filled all the house where they were sitting. And there appeared to them tongues as of fire, distributed and resting on each one of them. And they were all filled with the Holy Spirit and began to speak in other tongues, as the Spirit gave them utterance.

- ACTS 2:1-4

Pray 1 "Our Father" – 10 "Hail Marys" – 1 "Glory Be"

Prayer:

Jesus, Your disciples
received the Holy Spirit
to foster their love for You.
Grant that I may show my love
for You by proclaiming
the Good News of salvation.
Amen.

FOURTH GLORIOUS MYSTERY

Fruit of the Mystery:
Grace of a Happy Death

The Assumption of the Blessed Virgin Mary

The voice of my beloved! Behold, he comes, leaping upon the mountains, bounding over the hills. My beloved is like a gazelle, or a young stag. Behold, there he stands behind our wall, gazing in at the windows, looking through the lattice. My beloved speaks and says to me: "Arise, my love, my fair one, and come away; for lo, the winter is past, the rain is over and gone. The flowers appear on the earth, the time of singing has come, and the voice of the turtledove is heard in our land. The fig tree puts forth its figs, and the vines are in blossom; they give forth fragrance. Arise, my love, my fair one, and come away. O my dove, in the clefts of the rock, in the covert of the cliff, let me see your face, let me hear your voice, for your voice is sweet, and your face is comely."

- SONG OF SOLOMON 2:8-14

Pray 1 "Our Father" – 10 "Hail Marys" – 1 "Glory Be"

Prayer:

Mary, you were assumed
body and soul into heaven
by the power of God,
and united with your Divine Son, Jesus.
Obtain eternal happiness with Him for me.
Amen.

FIFTH GLORIOUS MYSTERY

Fruit of the Mystery:
Trust in Mary's Intercession

The Coronation of the Blessed Virgin Mary

And a great portent appeared in heaven, a woman clothed with the sun, with the moon under her feet, and on her head a crown of twelve stars; she was with child and she cried out in her pangs of birth, in anguish for delivery. And another portent appeared in heaven; behold, a great red dragon, with seven heads and ten horns, and seven diadems upon his heads. His tail swept down a third of the stars of heaven, and cast them to the earth. And the dragon stood before the woman who was about to bear a child, that he might devour her child when she brought it forth; she brought forth a male child, one who is to rule all the nations with a rod of iron, but her child was caught up to God and to His throne, and the woman fled into the wilderness, where she has a place prepared by God, in which to be nourished for one thousand two hundred and sixty days.

- REVELATION 12:1-6

Pray 1 "Our Father" – 10 "Hail Marys" – 1 "Glory Be"

Prayer:

Mary, you humbled yourself before God and you were crowned Queen of Heaven. Bless me with the love of the Holy Trinity and intercede for me in Heaven. Amen.

Prayers of the Rosary

The Apostles' Creed*

I believe in God, the Father almighty, Creator of heaven and earth, and in Jesus Christ, his only Son, our Lord, who was conceived by the Holy Spirit, born of the Virgin Mary, suffered under Pontius Pilate, was crucified, died, and was buried; he descended into hell; on the third day he rose again from the dead; he ascended into heaven, and is seated at the right hand of God the Father almighty; from there he will come to judge the living and the dead. I believe in the Holy Spirit, the holy catholic Church, the communion of saints, the forgiveness of sins, the resurrection of the body, and life everlasting. Amen.

Our Father

Our Father, who art in heaven; hallowed be Thy name; Thy kingdom come; Thy will be done on earth as it is in heaven. Give us this day our daily bread and forgive us our trespasses as we forgive those who trespass against us, and lead us not into temptation; but deliver us from evil. Amen.

*The wording of the Apostles' Creed conforms with the *Roman Missal*.

Hail Mary

Hail Mary, full of grace. The Lord is with thee.
Blessed art thou among women, and blessed is
the fruit of thy womb, Jesus. Holy Mary, Mother
of God, pray for us sinners, now and at the hour
of our death. Amen

Glory Be to the Father

Glory be to the Father, and to the Son, and to the
Holy Spirit. As it was in the beginning, is now,
and ever shall be, world without end. Amen.

Hail, Holy Queen

Hail, Holy Queen, Mother of Mercy, our life,
our sweetness, and our hope; to thee do we cry,
poor banished children of Eve; to thee do we
send up our sighs, mourning and weeping in this
vale of tears; turn, then, most gracious Advocate,
thine eyes of mercy towards us, and after this,
our exile, show unto us the blessed fruit of thy
womb, Jesus. O clement, O loving, O sweet
Virgin Mary! Pray for us, O holy Mother of
God, that we may be made worthy of the
promises of Christ.

How to Pray the Rosary

1. Make the Sign of the Cross and say the "Apostles' Creed."
2. Say the "Our Father."
3. Say three "Hail Marys."
4. Say the "Glory be to the Father."
5. Announce the First Mystery; then say the "Our Father."

For each of the 5 decades:

6. Say ten "Hail Marys," while meditating on the Mystery.
7. Say the "Glory be to the Father."

After each decade:

8. After each decade say the following prayer requested by the Blessed Virgin Mary at Fatima:
   "O my Jesus, forgive us our sins, save us from the fires of hell. Lead all souls to Heaven, especially those in most need of Thy mercy."
9. Announce the Second Mystery: then say the "Our Father." Repeat 6, 7, and 8 and continue with the Third, Fourth, and the Fifth Mysteries in the same manner.

Closing Prayer:

10. Say the "Hail, Holy Queen" after the five decades are completed.

When to Pray the Mysteries

The Joyful Mysteries are prayed on Mondays and Saturdays and are optional on Sundays during Advent and the Christmas Season.

The Luminous Mysteries are prayed on Thursdays.

The Sorrowful Mysteries are prayed on Tuesdays and Fridays and arc optional on Sundays during Lent.

The Glorious Mysteries are prayed on Wednesdays and Sundays.

Notes

Notes

Notes